# METAMORPHOSIS

## The Journey

**ANNETTA DRUMMOND**

**METAMORPHOSIS THE JOURNEY**
Copyright © 2024 by Annetta Drummond
Print ISBN – 978-1-954755-94-9

All rights reserved. No parts of this publication may be reproduced, or transmitted in any form or by any means, without prior permission of the copyright owners – except– for brief quotations used in reviews. Any unauthorized copying of this work could lead to civil liability and criminal prosecution. No part of this book may be produced, stored in a retrieval system, or transmitted by any means without the written permission of the author.

Published by:
Restoration of the Breach without Borders
133 45th Street, Building A7 West Palm Beach, Florida 33407
restorativeauthor@gmail.com
Tele: (475) 233-9008

**NOTE:** All Bible scriptures in this book are quoted from the New King James Version of the Bible, except otherwise stated.

**DISCLAIMER**

Neither the publisher nor the author is engaged in rendering professional advice or services to the reader. The ideas, suggestions, and procedures in this book are not intended as a substitute for seeking professional guidance. Neither the publisher nor the author shall be held liable or responsible for any loss or damage allegedly arising from any suggestion or information contained in this book. The author has exercised her freedom of expression, and the views of the author may not necessarily be those of the reader.

Memory may fail us at times and although this book is based on true stories, the author acknowledges that each event referred to in their respective chapters attempts to recall the events of their lives as accurately as possible.

# **DEDICATION**

With a heart filled with joy and gratitude to God my Father, I dedicate this short epistle of my becoming to the body of Christ in the earthly realm.

Also, I cannot but dedicate this epistle to everyone who is still in bewilderment regarding the way out of the grasp of the enemy and genuinely seeking to bring their divine assignment and purpose on the earth to fruition. I have been commanded to bring this unbending truth to you. And I did because I am nothing but a bondservant.

# Table of Contents

| | |
|---|---|
| Dedication | iv |
| Acknowledgments | vi |
| Testimony | viii |
| Introduction | xiii |
| Chapter 1: The Butterfly | 1 |
| Chapter 2: Understanding The Metamorphosis of Your Life | 7 |
| Chapter 3: You Have Never Been Alone | 16 |
| Chapter 4: The Power of God To Go And Become | 27 |
| Chapter 5: Built To Last | 35 |
| Chapter 6: How it Started | 45 |
| Chapter 7: Miracle Baby | 53 |
| Chapter 8: Bleeding | 60 |
| Chapter 9: Missions | 66 |
| Chapter 10: Attacks | 74 |
| Chapter 11: Launch Out | 92 |
| Chapter 12: Covid | 101 |
| Conclusion | 109 |
| About the Author | 112 |

# Acknowledgments

Unreservedly I owe so much to my husband and my children. The calling of God on my life has had a profound impact on them, just as it has on me. While He processes me, He processes them. Together, we are becoming. They have stood by me throughout my difficult encounters, life-draining moments, and wilderness days. Dervin Drummond, my husband was by me through it all, he demonstrated the qualities of a good man and one I will treasure for my lifetime, and if there be anything like a second time on the earth; I am still going to jump into his hands again as his wife. You are an immense gift to humanity and an epitome of a good husband, father, and God lover. Thank you for supporting me in it all and still standing by me. I love you.

My children: Andrè, Andrew, Athena, Anika, and Alexia Drummond; my unique 5A's, you all have played your part so distinctly well and have proven to be a source of inexplicable joy to me. By God's grace upon your individual lives, you have been instrumental to diverse good times and winning moments in my life. You guys are awesome. Nothing on this earth, above and beneath is worthy of being equated to your place and value in my life. Except God.

What can I say to all the persons I am connected to, my friends, and everyone God has sent to lift my head in those days when I was almost throwing the towel on my calling, purpose, and assignments? When I concluded, they said you are just getting started. With their time they supported me, with their counsel they guided me through, in their anointing they held me high, with the resources they gave to my assignment. Their professional and divine aid has brought me to the point where I can now scream SELAH!

My scars are testaments of God's tangible presence in the affairs of men. He has used you all to bless me. So, I declare generational blessings will pursue you and overtake you in this life, thereby making you an envy of your world.

# Testimony

When Apostle contacted me to edit her already-written manuscript, *"Metamorphosis The Journey"*, without hesitation I commenced. Subsequently, she sent me additional detailed information to be inserted. One morning, while driving with my three children, my phone fell out of the car and was shattered on the highway. This occurrence was strange as I was not holding it; it was kept in my bag. I can't explain how the bag got unzipped and my phone fell out on the highway while the car was at full speed. It's all very puzzling. Interestingly, the night before my husband said, "Honey please send all the untouched information Apostle had sent you to my WhatsApp" which I did. "I realized that God was ensuring that the Apostle's book information wouldn't get lost in any way." The deadline we gave to Apostle for finishing her book passed, therefore, my husband increased his commitment and speed in the pursuit of its completion.

As he worked on the book from his laptop, he was being ministered to. Every line Apostle wrote ushered him into deep thinking. Occasionally, as he worked on her book's content, I found him crying. I was shocked the first time, so, I asked him what the problem was, and he said: "God is amazingly mighty". I said, "But we know that so why are you crying?" He replied, "God is so eager to reveal Himself to anyone who will open up to Him, in the same dimension He has revealed Himself to Apostle Annetta numerous times". My husband was born again with various bible school certificates, but during the times of Apostle's book, his prayer life and spiritual responsibilities increased.

The phone was already shattered, and the deadline was missed. As if that wasn't enough, my husband's new laptop from a client in the United States suddenly stopped working. It had been working perfectly fine until that morning when it refused to turn on. My husband was very frustrated and didn't know what to do. Then my husband said to me that some forces do not want this book to be published.

We called a computer technician to come and check our laptop. He came over and thoroughly checked it, but he told us that everything was fine with the laptop.

However, he was unable to determine why the laptop was not turning on. Suddenly, my husband decided to end the inspection, paid the technician, and asked him to leave. When he left, my husband carried the laptop to his small altar in the house and knelt. He placed the laptop in front of him and said, "God the revelation and information in this book will transform lives and build churches into spiritual maturity. If you are the one who had asked Apostle Annetta to write this book to accomplish your will, then please make this laptop work". He left the laptop on the altar, took a shower, got dressed, and then carried the laptop back to his office, turned it on and it came on. We were flabbergasted. My husband talks about Apostle Annetta every day, indicating his attachment to her.

The enemy tried another stunt. This time he used an elderly couple, our neighbors who attend the same church as my family and me. They shouted and attacked us physically, followed by threats of spiritual attacks. Additionally, they accused my husband of spreading lies and gossip about them.

We were so shocked! This couple never offended us before. We were never friends but maintained amicable neighborly greeting terms. My husband and I are both writers and work from home. We rarely leave the house except to take our children out for some fun, attend church, or go for personal evangelism.

My husband tried to resolve the situation and asked the church to intervene but was advised by a pastor to allow the malice that had begun since the attacks commenced to take its course. Therefore, my husband decided that we should leave our house and rent another place. He also wanted us to leave our church because he couldn't appreciate malice between members. We lacked the financial resources needed to relocate to a nice place, therefore, we were forced to remain. This has affected my husband emotionally and has hampered his usual professional work speed on Apostle's book.

We know God will use it to transform lives, heal broken hearts, and give hope to people around the world. This book, as it helped my husband to come into a closer walk with God, will also help many to identify their failures and try again. The revelation in it has given expression to the purpose of men and women.

**Mr. and Mrs. Prince Agidi**
**Owners of El Shaddai Pen Academy and Global Kingdom Writers.**

# Introduction

We are not following cunning devised fables of men, for our God is mighty to save and mighty to deliver. What His mouth has pronounced, His hands are more than able to bring it to pass. This is the only key ingredient and revelation you need to have, to keep metamorphosing without aborting or contaminating the process yourself. The same is the required mindset needed for the race of your destiny in this lifetime. It is the catalyst to making your time on the earth to fulfill your God-given assignment is essential to receiving the honor from your creator by hearing Him say to you: well, done, thou faithful servant; you have fought the good fight of faith.

Metamorphosis, in a general sense, refers to a deep transformation or change in form, nature, or character. It is often used to describe a dramatic and sometimes unexpected change, typically associated with biological processes, literature, and psychology. In biology, metamorphosis commonly refers to the course undergone by some creatures as they develop from one stage to another, such as the transformation of a caterpillar into a butterfly or a tadpole into a frog. This biological metamorphosis involves distinct stages and often involves significant changes in physical structure, behavior, and habitat. In literature, metamorphosis commonly denotes themes of transformation, renewal, and rebirth. It can represent a change in identity, perspective, or circumstance, often leading to personal growth or enlightenment.

*"Metamorphosis The Journey"* is simply the stages and phases God and life will carry you through to becoming who God has predestined you to be. The word predestined means predetermined, which suggests that who you are, is already decided by God but not yet known by you. Your life's journey is the pathway to discovering who you are in Him.

As we journey through the pages of *"Metamorphosis The Journey"*, I will be using my true-life story and several supernatural, hard-to-believe first-hand encounters in my life to help you engage your purpose and cause it to find full expression no matter the obstructions standing before you. On this journey; there will be painful scars, heartbreaks, cuts, bruises, battering, and betrayals. You will be lied to/upon and falsely accused; mistreated, misunderstood and underestimated by others. During the journey of life, there will be certain times when you may feel lonely and that no one understands what you are experiencing. Additionally, various traumatic experiences may also appear unexpectedly and have a negative impact on you. However, it is important to remember that during this journey, God's presence will always be with you, guiding you through your transformation. For God said and I paraphrase: *"I know the thoughts and plans I have for you, to prosper you and to give you a good end."*

God is there in the valley and on the mountaintop with you. *"For He will never leave you nor forsake you."* Hebrews 13:5. I traveled through the wilderness and even encountered many obstacles, but with God's help, I made it through the desert and came out stronger. However, the journey was not easy, and I stumbled many times due to self-sabotage, as no one had shown me what I was about to reveal to you. Subsequently, I reached dead ends several times on this journey and I cried. My scars are a reminder of God's might and love for mankind.

"This journey will reveal to us who is on the Lord's side and who is not. Along the way, we will encounter both friends and foes. The obstacles that come our way may try to harm us, but they will only make us stronger."

The hell the enemy sent our way was basically to keep us from becoming what has been predestined for us to become in the earthly realm. As Christians, we can accomplish incredible things on this earth. We have the potential to dominate systems and politics. However, this can only be achieved if we allow the Lord to work in us and have faith in the process. Through our journey of metamorphosis, we can become the best version of ourselves.

The enemy uses our mistakes, inabilities, and negligence to sabotage us as he did with me for a very long time until I came to the fullness of the Godhead in me. Then I knew I had already finished the journey before I began.

*COME WITH ME ON MY JOURNEY AS I TAKE YOU THROUGH MY METAMOPHOSIS.*

# Chapter 1
# The Butterfly

We often see beautiful butterflies, but we rarely stop to consider the transformations they went through to beautify our world and pollinate the seeds of various plants. Butterflies are found in every land space across the world, except Antarctica, with over 18,000 species known to exist. The butterfly is a symbol of transformation, growth, and renewal in many spiritual traditions and cultures around the world. It often symbolizes hope and resilience, as it emerges from its cocoon despite the challenges it faces. Butterflies encourage us to embrace uncertainties and move forward. Just as the caterpillar must release its attachment to its old form to become a butterfly, we must be willing to separate ourselves from negative or old beliefs, habits, or relationships that no longer serve our highest good.

Before every butterfly became a butterfly, it went through four specific changes. Those changes are the needed transformation it must pass through to become what it was born to be. Without transformation, manifestation will never be realized.

The first stage of transformation is the egg stage. All butterflies start as tiny eggs each about the size of a pin which the female butterfly deposits on leaves in small clusters. Eggs typically gestate for about a week or two, at which point they hatch into butterfly larvae (caterpillars). The egg is only an egg to the ordinary eye, however, it's more than an egg. It is all that God designed it to fulfill. Hence, it moves from being an egg to the second stage- larva. Similarly, when a woman is pregnant, she is not merely carrying an unborn baby, but rather she is carrying purpose within her womb. The womb is not exempt from miracles. The Bible tells us in Luke 1 that John leapt in his mother's womb when he was in the presence of Jesus who was also a child in the womb. John was also filled with the Holy Spirit.

## METAMORPHOSIS THE JOURNEY

A minuscule caterpillar emerges from its egg. Its first meal typically consists of its eggshells. The caterpillar is built to devour, and it will consume a massive quantity of food before entering the pupal stage, increasing its body mass by thousands of times. Like the butterfly, the human must go through its stage of crawling. Many people struggle in this period due to the need for speed. Patience and timing are critical components to be embraced in this season.

The next stage of a butterfly's life cycle takes place inside a chrysalis (cocoon). While it may not look like much to the naked eye, there are incredible processes occurring in this motionless casement. During this processing, the caterpillar metamorphosizes into a butterfly but before then; for its safety and proper becoming; it must stay and remain inside its cocoon. Which is a protective shell, showing the sign that it is still in the process of becoming. At this stage, the butterfly is vulnerable to numerous attacks from predators, and therefore not many survive the process of actually becoming a butterfly. As a human, failure to be willing to cocoon which is time alone, learning

## Stages

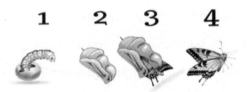

who we are, and pursuing who we are, will result in us not completing our process of metamorphosizes.

Each of the four stages of the butterfly's metamorphosis teaches powerful life lessons that we humans can tremendously benefit from.

Like the butterfly, humans must metamorphosis as we pursue intentionally the accomplishment of our destinies and purposes on Earth. God has created us to fulfill the assignment on our life for His good pleasures. Notwithstanding, we must go through stages and phases of life that will equip us to become who He has already created us to be.

If achieving destiny, manifesting purpose, and bringing vision to fruition were easy, everyone would do it in their strength. The record is there biblically and in our individual lives to substantiate the following claim- the Kingdom of Darkness will never make it easy for anyone who is striving towards the fulfillment of his or her God-given divine purpose. The devil knows that achieving your purpose is costly to him but enormously gainful to God and yourself. Additionally, he knows when purpose is fulfilled in one's life; the potential of lives to be impacted is unknown. One fulfilled life can easily equate to uncountable lives being rescued from the chaotic and destructive plans of the enemy, hence; he begins fighting one's destiny even before that one would come to the true understanding and knowledge of their purpose on earth.

According to Jeremiah 1:4-9,

*"Then the word of the Lord came to me, saying; behold I formed you in the womb I knew you; before you were born, I sanctified you; I ordained you a*

*prophet to the nations. Then said I; Ah, Lord God! Behold, I cannot speak, for I am a youth. But the Lord said to me: Do not say, I am a youth, for you shall go to all to whom I send you, and whatever I command you, you shall speak."*

For from the womb as the Lord picked Jeremiah and anointed him as prophet to nations, so also the devil will begin fighting a child of purpose and his assignment for God from the mother's womb. Therefore, parents must be cognizant of this truth- the enemy uses the mouth of parents to jeopardize their children's journey even before the journey begins for the child. Our words are powerful; and must never be addressed carelessly in the journey of metamorphosis.

# Chapter 2

# Understanding The Metamorphosis of Your Life

On this beautiful, intriguing journey called life, you will go through various chapters without your permission because your approvals are not needed for these phases to occur. Your responsibility is to comprehend each phase and positively maximize all possibilities. According to Philippians 1:6, the Lord will complete what He has started. Hence, God is easily classified as one of completion. If metamorphosis is not completed, the potential beauty of the pupa will never be manifested. Just like the caterpillar in the cocoon and the butterfly, so does the life of humans move through divinely orchestrated stages. These stages are orchestrated by God. Therefore, partnership with God is an investment in which true success in the earth and spirit realm resides.

The human who gets stuck in any of his/her transformational stages will never matriculate to the maximum possibility. It is therefore critically important that complete metamorphosis is pursued with maximum intentionality.

## **Enemy against Metamorphosis**

While we bask in the truth of metamorphosis, becoming who we are predestined to be, we are cautioned by the word of God according to 2 Corinthians 2:11, to not be novices to the devices of the enemy. In its pursuit to terminate or make of no effect, someone becoming as the kingdom of darkness targets specific stages.

We are dealing with a relentless devil. Who will never stop coming after us, especially when our assignment on the earth is so glorious and globally compelling, or will encourage people to turn to God? The enemy will come against everyone regardless of the size or nature of their assignment and to everyone who has decided to achieve God's reward and execute their divine mandate as to why they were born to the earth for God's glory. Predators come after the vulnerable butterfly when it is a pupa and a caterpillar in the cocoon, so also the devil comes for us when we are still in our cocoon stage or phase of life.

### *<u>Early stage</u>*

This is a significant period in the transformational journey. At this stage the enemy attacks with abortion. This is the willful termination of the fetus. There are many reasons why abortions are considered the preferred choice, notwithstanding, it is a weapon used effectively to kill possibilities.

Where abortion is scuffed at or attempted but failed, the next weapon used is miscarriage. This occurs when the unintentional termination of the fetus or baby is successful. When this is not achieved, the next option becomes stillbirth. The mother goes through the pain of labor and delivery, but the child is born dead.

Being persistent, the enemy sometimes causes parents to curse their children while they are still in their early stages. These curses begin as early as conception and are perpetuated throughout their lives if abortion, miscarriage, or stillbirth fails. To grasp this concept, we need to embrace this truth- Words are life or death. Parents negatively infect their children via words like, I never planned for this child, I never intended to have this child, or I am going to abort this child.

But hear what the Lord says:

*"For I know the thoughts that I think towards you, says the Lord, thoughts of peace and not of evil, to give you a future and a hope."* Jeremiah 29:11

### ***Attachments***

When a woman gets pregnant, it is as spiritual as it is physical. Many transactions take place, some without our physical knowledge. At this stage, words are powerful and very instrumental. Touch your stomach as a pregnant mother, irrespective of how the child came in there, and speak definite words for good to that child.

## *Scenario*

*Jane has three children, and she was going through an emotionally challenged period and found warmth in John's arms. She got pregnant and upon informing John, she was given money to have an abortion and John disappeared. She did not proceed with the abortion and nine months later she gave birth to her baby boy.*

Physically Jane goes through the pregnancy alone and experiences the changes in her body. After nine months were completed, she delivered. Spiritually, although abortion is not realized, the fetus gets infected by the spirit of rejection, abortion, and abandonment. Each of these comes with additional spirits, e.g., rejection comes with the spirit of fear and timidity.

## *Curse by names*

Names have meanings and extreme care must be given when a child is to be named. Just like the case of Jabez in the scriptures; the mother called him Jabez, meaning I bore him out of pain and Jabez's life was a shadow of himself because he was contaminated right in his mother's womb during his metamorphosis; even before he came to the earth to begin his journey.

*"Now Jabez was more honorable than his brothers, and his mother called his name Jabez, saying, because I bore him in pain."* 1 Chronicles 4:9

Though he was more honorable than his brethren during his metamorphosis in his journey, there was contamination that the enemy brought in through his mother in his cocoon stage, but he knew not.

Jabez was not a baby when he cried out unto the Lord, he was grown. Yet the pain of his reality continued. Jabez asked for enlargement. We have the power to change the trajectory of our lives. Like the butterfly, even when it eventually gets passed through its metamorphosis in its journey to becoming a butterfly; a snake can still have it for a meal if it ever is careless and not watchful. So, the enemy of our destiny and our assignment can derail us from our assignment, therefore we must be intentional and committed to the Lord.

Be confident in this wise-If the devil attacks God's destined ones from the womb, that means God protects His own from the womb also.

*"For you formed my inward parts; you covered me in my mother's womb. I will praise you, for I am fearfully and wonderfully made; marvelous are your works, and that my soul knows very well. My frame was not hidden from you, when o was made in secret, and skillfully wrought in the lowest parts of the earth. Your eyes saw my substance, being yet unformed. And in your book, they all were written, the days fashioned for me, when as yet there were none of them."* Psalms 139:13-16

### ***Parental responsibility***

As parents even if you feel you don't need the child, speak well of that child because he or she has come not because of you but because God designed them to come for His purpose not your purpose, speak positive things over the unborn child in your womb. Speak deliberate words like we will not abort this destiny because our words are powerful and they are like arrows when they go off from our mouth, we cannot retrieve them.

You have seen the vulnerable stages of your child during your child's metamorphosis into becoming the real person God has predestined him or her to be. We need to speak words of wisdom, words of love, and words of God over our children. Those words form a strong cocoon which is the protective shell for that child against the devil. I want to believe there is already some sort of awakening to responsibility to ensure the protection of that child's life, destiny, and purpose in their cocoon stage; in your womb, even before they are born into the world because the devil has begun his job already, the day you conceived.

Standing in the gap and speaking on behalf of your child can be challenging but necessary. A lot of people who are going through the process of their metamorphosis to become who God called them to be, find many things challenging. In these situations, they need to stand on the promises of God. Always remember, while in our mother's womb, He has called us into a purpose for His Kingdom, in a time such as this. As we are transformed, we will become the real version of ourselves and walk the earth like Jesus.

In understanding the metamorphosis of our lives, you must get to know that nothing is ordinary. As we develop daily into full-grown men and women more care should be given to our spirit being because it is the changes that occur there that manifest in our physical lives. Just like it is easy to get rid of a child in its embryonic stage; it is also easy to infect or kill a butterfly when it is in its egg, larva, or pupa stage because it cannot fly at this stage. Therefore, it becomes pivotal to tabernacle with God in prayer, fasting, and biblical counsel to ensure whatever had been injected into your destiny to hinder the full expression of your purpose in its appointed time might be revealed to you and be made to come to naught. So that the true manifestations of your purposes will be made known.

Our purpose moves us to come alive, it's the driving force as to why we get out of bed in the mornings. It's the motivator for the things we do daily. When our purpose is clear; it increases focus and ignites passion. Purpose builds resilience. There will be challenges along the way but no matter how many times we are knocked down, purpose will give you that grace to get back up and push forward. Let's live our lives purposefully.

# Chapter 3
# You Have Never Been Alone

*"Let your conduct be without covetousness; be content with such things as you have. For He Himself has said, I will never leave you nor forsake you."*
*Hebrews 13:5*

Our human limitations have clouded our understanding of the truth that we are never alone. Sometimes you see a child clinging to his or her parents, not wanting anyone to carry them due to fear. Not knowing that even if they allow another to carry them, they are still not alone because their parents are still present. So, it is with many of us. In our worst moments, we tend to feel like God has left us, which is not true. We only need to open our spiritual eyes to see Him.

It is comforting to know that God will never leave nor forsake us in a world that is constantly changing, where people come and go in our lives, whether they be family, friends, relationships, or even through death. It is very comforting to know that God promises never to leave or forsake us. All we have to do is trust Him.

The promise of 'I will never leave you or forsake you was given to Joshua and the Israelites before entering the promised land. (Deuteronomy 31:6)

Moses encouraged Joshua as his succeeding leader, reminding him that the Lord Himself goes before him and will be with him. Moses reminded Joshua not to be afraid or discouraged. Joshua's task of leading the children of Israel to the Promised Land seemed impossible, but with God on his side, the task was made possible.

At salvation, we are permanently indwelt with the Holy Spirit of God. Christ Himself affirmed that the Comforter (Holy Spirit) will be with us always (John 14:16). He will never leave, forsake, abandon, or leave us alone. We can live unbothered and unafraid because of this promise. We are never alone.

The glorious manner of Jesus's conception and birth was prophesied by Isaiah many years before its manifestation. Yet, at the time of prophetic fulfillment, there were many challenges and attempted murder of the baby Jesus. The problems began with Joseph thinking Mary deceived him and was prepared to cancel their marriage and put her away. This could easily have resulted in her being stoned to death. God intercepted his plan by speaking to him in a dream, letting him know, her pregnancy was of the Holy Spirit. Joseph obeyed the angel and took Mary as his wife.

After Jesus' birth, King Herod having heard that the King of the Jews was born, made a decree that all male children two years old and younger must be killed. This he did primarily to kill Jesus. God again warned Joseph in a dream telling him to flee to Egypt with Mary and Jesus. Sometime later, an angel visited

Joseph again and told him that it was safe to return because Herod was now dead.

At thirty years old, at the inception of His ministry, after He was baptized by John, a voice from Heaven confirmed that Jesus was the son of God. Then He was led by the Holy Spirit to be tempted by the devil in the wilderness. Jesus never gave in to the temptations of the enemy. Subsequently, the devil left Him, and angels came and ministered unto Him. James 4:7

Three and a half years later, Satan showed up again and influenced the crucifixion of Jesus. When Jesus was on the cross, he cried in agony, "And about the ninth hour Jesus cried with a loud voice, saying, Eli, Eli, lama sabachthani? that is to say, My God, my God, why hast thou forsaken me?" Mathew 27:46

From Jesus was in the womb, we see that He was never alone. God orchestrated His protection and survival. As an adult, we see also God being with Him throughout His life. The theory of us never being alone is challenged by the words Jesus cried when He was on the cross.

Jesus took on the sins of the world. He carried and felt the weight of sin which leads to separation. The cry of why hast thou forsaken me, prophetically is what those who have not accepted the sacrifice He did, will also utter. Please understand that according to John chapter 1, God and Jesus are one. Being one, separation was impossible. Jesus was never alone.

## ***My Experiences***

I have had many experiences, both good and bad. These experiences have made my belief in God stronger. I am convinced that He is always present, even during chaos and catastrophes. "I have had many out-of-body experiences that I cannot share with people. They may think that I am lying. However, these experiences have served as proof of God's ever-present influence in human affairs. Occasionally I see myself in different countries I've never been to physically. I will find myself fighting, doing deliverances, and many other godly acts. I was terrified.

The truth that comforted me was, If God has chosen you for a divine purpose, He will stay with you throughout your journey. Once you understand this, you can overcome any obstacle that may arise on your path to fulfilling your purpose in this world.

### *Victory In the Spirit*

The first time it happened was when I had an ectopic pregnancy in the year 1993. I underwent surgery and did not know I wasn't supposed to shower. My church family was coming to see me at the hospital, so I took a shower. Unfortunately, the wound got infected.

When they arrived, we began conversing. There was another woman who was in another recovery room which was in front of mine. From my bed, I could observe her since the curtain was not closed. When she got into her bed, I noticed a dark aura in the room, but I didn't pay much attention to it. One of the members of my church who came to visit me went to encourage the lady and offer her comfort.

My church family left about 8:15 pm, and the dark presence attacked me physically around 9 pm. Although I was lying on the bed, I saw myself leaving the room, went up through the window, and exited the hospital. I continued going up until I got to the roof of the hospital then I found myself in my house. I didn't know what was happening to me. When I got to my house, I noticed that fleets of demons were behind me. Immediately my husband came outside the house and rushed me inside to rescue me from the demons and to ensure I was safe.

I knew the time my church family left the hospital but the time I got home in the out-of-body experience I didn't know. After being discharged from the hospital and arriving home, my children said, "I came home before in the spirit, and their dad came outside and was screaming Annetta you're home! You're home!" My kids said they came out looking at their daddy and thought to themselves, something was wrong with him. My husband said that when I came home in the spirit, he saw me climbing the stairs, holding my stomach and a fleet of demons behind me. He said, "Annetta, there are demons behind you." He put me in the room, ensured I was safe, and then fought off the demons.

I asked them what time all these things happened and when they told me 9 pm, I realized it was the same time the dark presence attacked me. That was when it became crystal clear to me that I had an out-of-body experience.

Both our bodies and spirits go through warfare. Physically, my body was weak and sedated so there was no way I could handle that warfare physically. I am certain that if God had not taken me out of the hospital I would have been defeated. I needed the help and strength of my husband to assist me in defeating the demons. To take me inside to rest from the weakness and excruciating pain I was experiencing from the wound.

God will be with you in your; dreams, when you are in a coma, or when you are in the theater undergoing surgery. God never leaves His own alone. Let this thought be in you and see how obstacles will turn into the ingredients that will invent your miracles. Trusting in God is a powerful weapon in the process of your metamorphosis; if you lose everything, do not lose your trust in God. No matter how many times you fail, and the situation gets worse; your trust in God is your shield in your cocoon stage and your shield even when eventually you make it to the stage of an actual butterfly because God never forgets or abandons His own.

He came to me in the form of a huge white eagle as big as a small plane. I stepped out of my body onto the back of this white eagle. It was like I was on my own private jet plane. The smell coming from the feathers of this eagle was out of this world. I buried my face in the feathers of the eagle close to his neck. I felt so peaceful, and the overwhelming love made me relinquish all of myself to this beautiful creature.

I was soaring and going up and about. There was no seat belt, but an invisible strap held me on the back of this magnificent bird. He took me into Heaven, which seemed like another dimension. All the flowers and grass were so bright and beautiful; unlike anything I have ever seen on Earth. I was in awe; I don't think I am doing justice in describing what I have seen.

He was taking me over the sea, and the different green and blue colors were spectacular. I looked down and noticed that the colors were getting darker, indicating that the sea was getting deeper and deeper.

Growing up in Jamaica, we usually went to the beach. My dad, who was an Able-Bodied Seaman, was like a fish in the water. He usually took us out where our feet couldn't touch the ground. He would immerse us in the water three times consecutively. I could hardly catch my breath and it felt like I was drowning. After that, he would let me go when my feet could touch the sand. I would run to the shore to my mom for safety.

I love the water and would go into it up to my waist, but if anyone touched me, I would panic because I felt like I was going to drown. This is the fear I felt as I was going over the water on this beautiful white eagle. I raised my voice and said, "JESUS! JESUS! Put me back!" and immediately I was back in my body. As I was settling down and thinking about the experience, I heard the Spirit of the Lord say to me, "You didn't trust your father not to drown you, so you don't trust me to take you over." I don't know what that "over" meant or even looked like, but I believe it was something out of this world.

As I was going over this experience in my head, I knew I had a trust issue. I wept like a baby, sat up in a chair at my bedside, and told God to come back; I have learned my lesson. I will trust Him. He never came back in that way again. Both truths run parallel. I didn't trust my earthly father not to drown me, therefore, I couldn't trust my Heavenly Father to take me over the water. Just like Peter, I started watching the depths of the water and lost focus on where I was going and who I was with.

The thing I feared to overcome is what kept me from crossing over to the other side. The scripture that came to mind is Ezekiel 47:4: "Again he measured a thousand, and brought me through the waters; the waters were to the knees."

While we can maneuver ourselves in the water, we can control situations. When we have to let go and trust someone else to take us through unfamiliar places and situations, it takes another level of trust.

Isaiah 26:3-4 You will keep in perfect peace, him whose mind is stayed is steadfast because he trusts in you. Trust in the Lord forever, for the Lord is the rock eternal.

# Chapter 4
# The Power of God To Go And Become

The devil started messing with me from a young age and I didn't know who I was, nor did I know what I was carrying. My self-esteem suffered greatly, leading me to shed many tears over the relentless battles and attacks. My life was filled with unanswered questions, unfortunately, there were no mentors to explain that I was being processed. I never knew I was going through my developmental stages, and no one told me how my reactions to these events would determine my outcome.

Even though I was filled with the Holy Spirit, I did not know Him intimately. I was just trusting my instincts. One scripture I hold onto that empowers me for my assignment here on earth is Luke 10:19: "Behold, I have given you power to tread on serpents and scorpions, and over all the power of the enemy; and nothing shall by any means hurt you."

God sends the Holy Spirit to empower us for the assignment, and our responsibility is to become who He has called us to be. Apostle Luke captured the words of Jesus which say, *"Behold, I give unto you power to tread on serpents and scorpions, and over all the enemy: and nothing shall by any means hurt you."* Luke 10:19(KJV)

Power is a commodity that can never be left aside when destiny is to be achieved and purpose is to be accomplished. Nobody said this road would be easy, but with Christ in the vessel; we can smile at the storm. In the metamorphosis that leads to our becoming; it will never be a smooth ride. The good news is the journey was already finished even before you decided to begin. All we are pursuing to achieve on the earth has already been deposited in us even before we set out to accomplish them. This truth was made clear to us from the scriptures:

*"For whom He foreknew, He also predestined to be conformed to the image of His Son, that He might be the firstborn among many brethren. Moreover, whom He predestined, these He also called; whom He called, these He also justified; and whom He justified, these He also glorified."* Romans 8:29-30

The power to become not only resides in knowing and understanding, but the application of the same is that which will lead to becoming who God has called you to be.

If you know God has called you for His assignment but you feel insufficient, do not become frustrated. You did not call yourself; God did. Hence, He will show you every step to take and align you with the right people who will come alongside you to help bring the vision to fruition.

Even after realizing the call of God was on my life, I was still reluctant to go forward. I had the Holy Spirit who is my guide. Notwithstanding, I never knew what God was empowering me to become.

Until the power of the Holy Spirit is released, you will never understand or operate in your divine office. This office isn't the kind you assume after an appointment letter/employment letter has been issued to you. You can only come into the fullness of your divine office when power has been given to you to become. Otherwise, nothing can bring you into your call and assignment. Let us never forget, *"A man can receive nothing unless it has been given to him from heaven."* John 3-27

It was the darkest of dark times of my life. I found myself counting my failures and focusing on my inabilities. I would not wish the experiences I endured during that time on anyone, not even on my enemy. I never knew the essence of God's power, nor did I know that power had already been given to me. Therefore, I struggled in my metamorphosis to become who God predestined me to be. Until you know and accept the truth that whatever God has given you and called you to do in the earthly realm, only He can fulfill it through you and bring it to pass on His terms, not on yours. This truth will cause you to surrender and when you yield to God; that is when He begins using you in His full will.

*"Let no one deceive himself. If anyone among you seems to be wise in this stage, let him become a fool that he may become wise."* 1 Corinthians 3:18

In Judges 6:12-14, Gideon encountered an angel who addressed him as a mighty man of valor and gave him the assignment to save his people. Gideon doubted the words of the angel because he saw himself as of no great esteem. Like Gideon, I was a woman of valor, but I was like a grasshopper before my eyes. I always ran to hide my wheat in the winepress because of the Midianites, my enemies. I seriously sabotaged myself without the help of anyone. When I was given a task; I would unconsciously give reasons why I was not capable. Subsequently, I retreated causing me to miss many heavenly-orchestrated opportunities. All that was required was my willingness to try, and God's hand would have accelerated me into progress resulting in the evasion of many delays. This, which I speak of, happens to many around the world and causes many destinies to be aborted or delayed.

Until Gideon realized might was in him, he was still running from the enemies who had the upper hand over him. This happens simply because we do not know that power had already been given to us to become whatever God had designed us to be in the earthly realm for His good pleasures. We need revelation to become anything worthy and to execute our purpose on earth. Additionally, we need power to dominate policies and systems for God.

Like many others, this knowledge was not known to me. As a result, I was feeling frustrated with the ministry. I noticed that every time I faced disappointment or setbacks, I felt like giving up, closing the door, and shutting down the church. One day God said to me: "You didn't start it, so you can't finish it." From that day, I decided I would keep on obeying God and doing what I was doing to the best of my abilities.

Whenever I felt unable to handle a situation, the Lord would send someone to lift my spirits and encourage me to keep pushing through, no matter how difficult the circumstances were. Even when we were struggling financially, the Lord sent persons to provide us with the necessary funds. These individuals were moved by God to sow into our lives and bless us with the money we needed, and sometimes even more.

"After realizing that I couldn't accomplish anything on my own, I became conscious of the importance of God's help. This realization led me to depend on God instead of myself. At the point of this revelation, the power of God, what your purpose requires will come and begin to bring your vision to fruition and the same power will cocoon you and envelop you. This is when you will begin to operate and walk in absolute power.

I came to an understanding that I carry the life of Jesus. I became confident in my ministerial operation and life generally. Then one day my daughter Athena said: **"Mummy you know, you are not afraid to fail, but you are afraid you might succeed and don't know what to do"**, that statement hit me straight in my spirit because I knew the Holy Spirit was the one speaking through her. She was right; I knew if I failed, I would shut it down but if I succeeded, I would feel inadequate. God used her words to revolutionize my outlook on life.

That experience shook me up and made me think on a deeper level. That was the moment I decided to hand over everything to God. I re-dedicated myself and the ministry to God and re-launched it the way it should have been launched. After that, I also gave my children and husband back to God. I said, 'God, I am not my own.' That was when I began to walk in the realm of the spirit with accuracy and precision, and the Holy Spirit helped me to fully understand my assignment. Then I realized who I am and whose I am."

Interestingly, my confidence increased because I started believing in myself. However, there was still some residue of low self-esteem in me. Something became evident in my life: whenever I came across a task that I was afraid of, God would send someone to encourage me to go on. I developed an awareness of the life of God in me. This was the metamorphosis in my journey to carrying the required power which caused me to become who I am today, and the same experience caused me to write this book to you.

*"But as many as received him, to them gave he power to become the sons of God, even to them that believe on his name."* John 1:12(KJV)

# Chapter 5
# Built To Last

It's your vision! It's your vision! I kept on hearing these words non-stop, I felt like I was going crazy.

I couldn't take it anymore so one morning after hearing these words in my head for almost a week, I said yes God! I heard you, not knowing that I involuntarily answered the call of God on my life.

This happened after I shared the vision with my friend telling her why the enemy was attacking our relationship with our pastor. Her response was it's not your pastor's vision, it is not your husband's vision! It's your vision. In this vision early one morning, the Lord transported my husband, my then pastor, and myself to a pinnacle and showed us the world without form, just vast darkness with only the earth's globe.

When I looked closely, I saw the hand of God under the earth like He was holding it up in His hands. Over the globe, I saw Global Deliverance Ministries.

My husband had just become a child of God, so I told my pastor that I saw the ministry that God had prepared for him. `I did not see myself in the equation because of where I was spiritually.

After I shared the vision with my pastor all hell broke loose. The enemy started attacking me from every angle even from my pastor and his family, and I just couldn't understand why!!! They would rally others on their side, and they too started coming against me. I was accused of lying and others were told not to be associated with me.

They now have others who were in alliance with them because of what was spoken about me. Whenever I made suggestions in any meeting it was outrightly dismissed, but later on, you would see the same suggestions being implemented as if it were someone else's ideas. I was mistreated and my name was constantly on their round table talks.

Who will believe little insignificant me above my pastor and his family? However, a young lady who was living with them came to me one day and said, 'I heard them speaking ill of you, yet I saw you constantly bringing things for them and being kind.

I wanted to get to know her for myself. She started taking me out for lunches and dinners where we would talk, and I would encourage her in her walk with the Lord. Trust started to develop between us. I began visiting her house to counsel her parents, who were very private and cautious about whom they spoke to. I eventually became her confidant to the point where she now calls me Mama. She became part of my family.

I was looked down upon at church, and some persons didn't want to associate with me. Even those who knew me were taking sides. If my husband said no to a request, it was assumed that I had told him to say no, as if I was controlling him or he didn't have a mind of his own. My husband is a very humble and quiet man. He's a man of his word; his yes is yes and his no is no, and he's not a pushover.

He loves me very much, almost as Christ loves the Church. He encourages me to fulfill the call of God on my life, supports me on my mission trips, covers me in prayer, and takes care of my expenses. He's a good father and grandfather to our five children and grandchildren. He stood with me when I felt abandoned and through all that I was going through. My husband is my rock and the love of my life.

The Lord didn't allow me to know that I was being abused so that my heart would remain pure towards them, even after hearing this from the young lady! It didn't change how I felt towards them, God had already placed a love in my heart for that family that even if I wanted to change it, it would not change.

After involuntarily accepting the call of God on my life, the voice stopped, so I continued my life as usual. I went into a very dark period of my life, one of the darkest moments I believed any human could have experienced. Many went through less than this and lost their minds but God. First, my parents who were living with me died a year and a half apart. That shook my whole world and that of my siblings. My mother was the matriarch of our family and after she died my family was never the same. My dad's death was a shock to me, there was nothing wrong with him, he just got up one day and left us to be with his true love, they had been together for over 50 years. I blocked my dad's death out because I didn't want to deal with it. I told myself that he was in Jamaica. I didn't get a chance to mourn my parents when my 1st born son met in an accident the following year. It was an ice storm on April 4, 2003, in Toronto Canada.

When the police came to my house and told me about my son's accident, he said, that of all the accidents that he was called to that day, my son was the only one who was alive. We called his wife to meet us at the trauma hospital, where we were all gathered in a room. They called the hospital's chaplain because they said my son was dying. The doctor told us to pull the plug because his brain was badly damaged and if he came out of the coma, he would be a vegetable. We refused to pull the plug. I said if God was going to take him, he would have died on the spot. Today he's talking and his memory is coming back and most of all he's alive. To God be the Glory because only He alone will get the Glory out of our lives.

During this period of darkness! My children turned away from God! Their reasons were why didn't God do something? Why didn't he stop the truck from hitting their brother? Why doesn't this God that we serve heal him? They had so many questions that I had no answers for! I was truly physically and emotionally exhausted. I felt like Job! Everything dear to me was gone; all I could do was praise God and pray! Pulling from the little strength I had.

Some of the rarest pearls are found in the deepest waters and some of His choicest servants are found in the darkest valley. It's in the valley He restores our soul. Two powerful verses that assisted me are Job 1:20, and Psalm 23:4: Even when I go through the darkest valley, I fear no danger, for you are with me, your rod and staff comfort me.

This was the hardest part of my journey that I had to go through and still going through, but my trust is in God only. In the process of my becoming, regardless of everything I've been through even in the darkest times of my life, I saw the hand of God helping and guiding me through the difficult season. I was going through my transformation and God ensured that nothing hindered my manifestation. This came about when that which was sent to break me only made me, I was built to last.

Those who are called to globally impact this world for the Kingdom of God, who have gone through their process are the ones who have accepted the call and become one with it. Knowing that it is not in our own strength but it's in the strength of The Lord. We cannot just sit back and say the Lord gave me a vision. From that vision was sent to you by God, it's already finished in the realm of the spirit. We are graced to make it happen in the earthly realm with the help of the Holy Spirit to impact the world we are living in.

In the book of Nehemiah, we see jealousy raging as purpose is being executed. "We built the walls, and the outer was joined together up to half of its height for the people had a mind to work. The key word is to have a mind to work, ministry doesn't come easy. It wasn't easy for Jesus, and it won't be easy for us.

There will always be the Samballats and the Tobias and their co-horst coming against you from all sides when you set out to do the work of the Lord. The enemy knows where God is taking us even before we do. Our story has already been written and God is working our lives into his plans for his good pleasure, therefore the devil starts devising his evil schemes to abort our destiny.

Although purpose cannot die, the enemy with his schemes can cause delays. If we're not careful of these traps, we can fall right into them. In the process of our delay, others whom we are assigned to will also be delayed in their process, however, if we can push past the pain of our uncertainties and trust the process, most of all trust God to bring us through. It will be glorious after this as He will use anything or anyone to help bring forth His glory through you.

When you come into your purpose, you are taking others to theirs as well. You are now anointed to do what He has called you to do. Be mindful that the anointing attracts good and bad therefore we have to guard what is in our lives with all our hearts. We've gone through so much to be here. It's like the oyster, the little grain of sand gets into its shell and irritates the oyster until it produces a precious pearl that what we carry is more precious than pearls.

If you find yourself going through traumas or negative experiences instead of delaying your process, seek help. Seek the Lord in fasting and prayer and seek biblical guidance from integral women and men of God. Whatever you do, no more delays.

God has already equipped and graced us to accomplish the assignment. That which seems like tragedy is strategic in the hands of God. He will turn it for our good.

We live in both worlds simultaneously, the spirit world where we live is more real than the physical world that we're passing through. If we can understand that then we can comprehend this occupy until he comes. Take dominion because this process is building and making us into His image.

This will enable us to start doing the ministry that we are called to do. I'm not just talking about the pulpit, there are a lot of ministries outside of the four walls of the church. There are no big ministries or small ministries. Some were called to lead God's people that's all, but we are all servants of the most High God.

Our ministry is for the perfecting of the saints and the edifying of the body of Christ all this is that we come into the fullness of Christ to be just like Him in this world. If we can catch that and become the best version of ourselves, we will avoid being shipwrecked.

**What He has called us for, we are well able and equipped to accomplish the will of God for our lives. We were built for this. We are built to last.**

# Chapter 6

## How it Started

I was born in Jamaica to a family of 9 siblings with both parents. My father was an able-bodied seaman so his work would take him all over the world. He would be away for four to six months at a time; he would come home and be with us for two to three weeks at a time. It saw our mother who raised us and when she became tired and frustrated, she would say wait until your father comes. That would straighten us out every time. Although Daddy didn't beat us like our mom, we were afraid of him.

Most Jamaican parents would send their children to Sunday school, and we were no different. We had to go and stay for midday service. I enjoyed going to Sunday school because we would get money to buy snacks. I also enjoyed entering competitions to win prizes from Sunday school like reciting the sixty-six books of the bible. To me, that was fun not knowing that the seed of the word of God was planted in me.

As I grew older church became uninteresting to me so I gradually found excuses why I couldn't go to Sunday school/ church.

This young man started pursuing me, he was so handsome and older than me, so I shunned him and didn't want anything to do with him. After about a year I eventually gave in to him. All this time my strict mother didn't know what was going on. I got pregnant at seventeen therefore, I didn't get a chance to finish high school. Upon learning about the pregnancy, my mother started treating me differently. She said, I wanted to be a woman, so she would treat me as such. After the baby was born, I started going to young people's meetings. There one Tuesday night the Lord called me, and I answered his call. At that time, I didn't think about the baby's father or anything at all. I decided to follow Jesus no matter what.

My baby's father and I were planning to get married at the end of that year. I was saved in March of the said year. We were so much in love and my baby's father wanted to do good by me, so we decided to elope. We got married on June fifteenth, 1980, one month shy of my nineteenth birthday. My family was not pleased because they were gearing up to have a big wedding in December. All my family from Canada was coming to Jamaica for my wedding so they were disappointed.

I got pregnant with my second child on my wedding night. My dreams of going back to school became slim with me being a married woman with two children. My education was pushed to the back of my mind. I was now focused on being the best wife and mother ever.

I started having prayer meetings in my house with the young people from church, I became like a leader/counsellor to them. For those who were getting married, I would prepare them with what to expect. It was at these prayer meetings most of the young people got filled with the Holy Spirit. We would see the hand of God and experience His tangible presence.

One particular moment stands out when we began praying with only a few of us while waiting for the others to join. One of the sisters began praying in English, then seamlessly transitioned into speaking in tongues. I was so filled with excitement that I immediately got up and hurried to call the others. One of the sisters shared with me that her mother had instructed her to complete her chores before doing anything else. I met her crying saying that she felt the presence of God come upon her in her bathroom and she couldn't stop crying. I ran back to the group and as soon as I entered my room. The presence of God was so present in the room that all I saw were thick white clouds! I tried to step on my floor, but it seemed like I was walking three feet above the ground. That day God showed up and these young people were strengthened, and their faith grew stronger.

With all of this going on my husband was not saved yet. My husband was a good man always providing for us and was there for his children to the best of his abilities. Because he was not saved yet there was a tug of war in the realm of the spirit with him going one way and I going another. The children would go to Sunday school at the church where I attended.

This caused me to be in constant prayers and so was the warfare fighting for the souls of my family. Although I had young people around me, I felt all alone. I could not burden them with my troubles. I had no one to talk to.

I got pregnant with my third child and things became harder for our young family. My husband tried everything he could lay his hands on to do. He started a flower shop, a restaurant, and a grocery store, but they all failed because he would give the less fortunate some if not most of the profits and therefore couldn't restock his inventory.

My parents were living in Canada and would assist us in whatever way they could. Every month they would send money to pay the mortgage and some to buy groceries for our family. This would last for a week or two. We struggled as a family, but I held on to my integrity. God was my source.

I could have made the mistake of aborting the plans of God for my life and the life of my family because there were rich men who offered proposals before and even after marriage. Understand this when we make moves contrary to the Word of God, we open the door to the enemy to destroy our lives. Not only destroy our lives but also abort our destiny and that of our families. I decided to Go God's Way. Times were hard and challenging but we decided to ride out the storms of life together. Whenever we met any challenges or what seemed like a dead end, we would see God our provider come through for us. Just like how he parted the Red Sea for the Israelites when they thought all was lost.

On seeing this my husband started going to church with me but every time he got close to God, the enemy would send someone to propose to him to record some reggae songs for them. He was a popular reggae artist in those days. It was easy for him to pull back into what was familiar and comfortable to him. This made me increase my intercession for him and my children who were getting older.

We eventually migrated to Canada and lived with my parents, this was not the ideal situation, but we were new to Canada and had no jobs yet. What made it worse was that I was pregnant with my fourth child.

With this, we decided to buy a house together. I worked with my mom in her day care and my husband worked in a flower shop. When we saved up enough to buy the house, we were so excited because the children could have their own space. After about two years later the bank manager told us we were not qualified for the mortgage. My mother pleaded our cause and told the bank manager that we had not missed a month's payment so how come he's saying we are not qualified? My parents were retirees, and we didn't have our papers yet. Technically we were not qualified but God made us house owners. To Him be all the glory and many other miracles we've experienced while in that house.

By this time, I was pregnant with my fifth child. She came under adverse circumstances and so I called her my miracle baby. More details on this will be in the next chapter.

I started going to church with my mother in Canada. Church was going well, and I was thriving until our pastor had to leave to pastor another ministry with his brother. I was heartbroken because I was now breaking out of myself. We got another pastor who started well but with time things started getting worse. It was at this point in my life when I started feeling the enemy coming after me to abort my purpose here on earth. This is how I learned warfare for my life and the life of my family.

My husband finally got saved after he had a miraculous encounter with God. We started building our altar together and God began ordering and directing our paths. Although I was not always obedient to God's nudges, I kept on pressing towards the mark of the higher calling in Christ Jesus Phillipins:3:14. Although he was a new Christian, I finally had someone to talk to and this gave me peace.

# Chapter 7
# Miracle Baby

I was in shock! I was on birth control. I slumped in the chair crying because I had already booked an appointment to get my tubes tied. I felt very sick, so I went to a doctor to see what was wrong with me. After running some tests, the doctor told me I was pregnant. I was pregnant with my fifth child, and once again the devil tried to abort my heritage. The first attack came when the doctor recommended me to an abortion clinic. I couldn't handle another child because I was mentally and physically exhausted. However, when I heard the word abortion, I immediately paid him and left. I never went back to him.

I started prenatal checkups with my obstetrician. After running some tests, he said he saw some abnormalities in the baby in the form of spina bifida.

This is a birth defect in which an area of the spinal column doesn't form properly, leaving a section of the spinal cord and the spinal nerve exposed through an opening in the back. The Doctor sent me to do an in-depth ultrasound at the Toronto General Hospital. This should determine what exactly is happening to my baby.

On the day of the appointment, all sorts of emotions ran through me, and being pregnant added to it. The medical stenographer finished the ultrasound and after the doctor read the results, the nurse told me that everything looked good. However, they could not be sure until they withdrew fluid from my baby's spine and examined it. She said it is a possibility that the baby could be aborted. When I heard about abortion again, I told her I would not go through with the next procedure.

I walked down the street crying and with all strength departed from me, I held onto my husband who gave me his strength. I said to God, "God you know that I cannot handle a special needs child, I can't even manage what I have furthermore I'm not legal in this country yet."

After I went home, I called my original pastor's wife, as we were good friends. I told her what was happening, and she organized a 24-hour prayer meeting. Everyone who was invited to join the prayer session chose a time that was convenient for them to pray. Out of this prayer group, the church grew stronger. Various testimonies came forth from people saying that they were healed and delivered. Some testified that before they didn't have a prayer life and now, they have a prayer life all because of the SOS that went out for our baby. I rested assured that prayers were going up for me and my family and angels were on assignment.

One night when I was about 6 months pregnant, the children were asleep, and my parents and my husband went to church. I had a dream that I saw a beautiful woman playfully jumping over a little stream. She did this three times but the third time I saw a big black hand pull her down into the water. She was down there for a while, and I spoke to God as if He was right there beside me; "God she cannot be alive" The Father said to me, "The devil possessed that body." They found the body later down the stream and in the funeral procession, while the body was in the coffin, I saw the woman sitting on top of her coffin teasing and laughing at the Christians. No one was able to see her but me. I said to myself, I was not going to engage in any spiritual warfare because she was not troubling anyone. As if she was reading my mind, she started terrorizing my family. I went to my pastor in Jamaica and asked him for some olive oil or holy blessed water so I could throw it on the woman. By this time, she presented herself as an angel of light. So, when I showed my pastor her, he said, "No she's not a demon." I took the water and threw it on her. Not being assured of my authority, I said "In the name of Jesus!" She laughed at me, and said, "A suh u do it?" (That's how you do it?) Immediately a righteous indignation rose in me and this time I said with all the assurance knowing who I am in Christ Jesus, "IN THE NAME OF JESUS CHRIST OF

NAZARETH" and I threw the water in her face. She slithered on the ground and turned into half an alligator and half an animal with fangs and long nails. I went closer to her to finish what I started, and she pushed one of her nails inside my vagina touching my baby. I screamed out because of the pain I felt in my physical body.

The pain woke me up from this ever-so-real dream. I started bleeding so much that blood gushed down my feet. I called my pastor's wife and told her what happened, and she prayed for me and the child. She called her husband who told my husband, and he came home and took me to the hospital. After examining me the doctor said my womb was low and that was what was causing the bleeding. I knew what had happened to me that night, so I thanked him and went home.

There were two more attempts on my baby's life. The first one I dreamt that there was a baby on the floor of my house looking uncared for and I felt sorry for it. I didn't have a good feeling about the baby, but I let my caring emotions take over. I bent down to pick up the child and the baby ran up my foot into my vagina went straight to my womb and tried to pull my baby out. My baby ran under my heart and that's when the demon baby disappeared. The other was when I was about 7 months pregnant. My sister asked me to babysit my little nephew for her. While he was sleeping in my arms, I saw a tall white man peep into my room and say, "Oh that's not the baby we want."

All this time prayers were being made on our behalf. When it was time to deliver my purpose, I was a little nervous, but I trusted God. When she was born, she was without any special needs or spine bifida. All I did was rejoice in the God of my salvation, He did it again! Only He alone will get the glory out of our lives.

Our daughter was saved at 4 years old and literally begged to be baptized. She was baptized at 7 years old; the Lord has chosen her from in my womb to do great works in the kingdom of God.

# Chapter 8

## Bleeding

Unlike the woman with the issue of blood recorded in Luke 8:43-48, whose bleeding was physical, mine was emotional and mental. I was bleeding but still going to church and serving, that's all I knew to do because God put a love in my heart for his people and I desire to see them whole. He never allowed me to have any kind of animosity towards those who abused or mistreated me because He was carrying me.

I served the ministry that I was under and honoured my leaders. This was instilled in me from my church in Jamaica where the foundations were made on the fundamentals of the Word of God. I was taught not to speak against the church pastor or leaders in general. That's why I was abused and did not know that I was being abused. I thought it was the norm.

So, I served even when I was being abused and did not understand what I was doing. I merely did what I was told. I served while disappointed and crying. Despite all these emotions I still pushed past the pain. Anything that was given to me to do, I did wholeheartedly, that's how God wired me. This is a principle I have insisted that my children adopt. Whenever they performed their chores poorly and I asked them to redo them, I would remind them to do it right the first time to avoid having to do it again. I stuck to that motto.

I was bleeding but ministering, carrying, and pushing others and they would get their deliverance and I am left bleeding.

In all of this, I kept on trusting in God's tender care and his favours. Just like Joseph in prison, he was locked up not knowing his fate, but he was still serving. I was locked up in my prison and couldn't even share it with my husband because he was a new Christian. I didn't want to contaminate his spirit with all that I was going through. " To him that is pure, all things are pure but the defile and unbelieving nothing is pure. Titus 1:5. My husband was so pure because he encountered God when he was getting saved in his bed, so I wanted him to stay that way.

I was being processed by God, but I didn't know it nor did I understand what was happening to me. There were no mentors to come alongside to help me realize what was happening to me. So, I fought everything that came my way. At this point, I didn't trust anyone because those who should protect and help me develop into who God called me to be, had their agenda. Therefore, I fought in prayer and attitude, and sometimes I talked back.

Frustration led me into my prayer closet where I found solace in communicating with God. My prayer life started developing and I started having vivid dreams and experiences with God. Although all this was happening to me, I didn't have anyone I could share it with but my husband.

I started evolving and somewhat started believing in myself. I still sabotage myself because of my lack of education, which I used as an excuse not to launch out into the deep. I was comfortable where I was because I could navigate the shallow waters of my life. I had to quickly learn that God does not want me to be in charge of my life as He is the author and finisher of it.

I was timid like Gideon but was anointed and didn't know it. There were a lot of prophecies over my life as to who God says I am! I was tired of people saying what God says, therefore, I locked myself into my closet in prayer asking God who am I?

An apostle from Detroit started mentoring me and he seemed like the only one who understood me. We met on February 14, 2014, and by April I was in Detroit ministering at one of his big conferences. He just wouldn't take no for an answer because he saw greatness in me that I couldn't see in myself. I started believing a little more in who I am. He had another conference in Atlanta Georgia and when I saw the big names on the flyer, I begged him to use someone else, but he refused again because he believed in my God-given gifts and talents and was not intimidated by anyone being used by God.

I ministered as I was commanded by the Lord, all this time still bleeding. I was still suffering from low self-esteem, but I refused to let go of the One who has called and ordained me from the foundation of the world to bring forth his praise and glory.

During this period, God bottles our tears and prevents us from bleeding out. Like the woman with the issue of blood, by faith, she reached out and touched the hem of Jesus' garment and immediately her issue stopped. She was desperate and out of desperation she got up with whatever little strength she had. She had forgotten about the Mosaic Law that says she was unclean and whoever touches her shall be unclean as well until the evening. She had a need that could cost her life.

I can relate to this woman, and I didn't have to walk a mile in her shoes to realize I share her path. I did not have a blood issue, but our life circumstances were not vastly different.

We all have things that we struggle with for years, whether it be health or heartbreak. The loss of a loved one or an ongoing situation that we can't seem to overcome. This drains our emotions, our strengths, and our time. For me, over the years I was drained of every ounce of strength in me. I had to pull on that strength and touch from the Lord. I realized that every day is an opportunity to live, and I was grateful to God for sustaining me. I realized for me to move forward I will have to let go of the past and take hold of my future.

When I acted on this revelation the bleeding stopped.

# Chapter 9

## Missions

I knew that this was God. I was so excited because I've been praying about missions. One of my friends from our church asked me if I wanted to go on a trip to Ethiopia with her professor from the bible school she was attending. The mission was scheduled for the 15 of September. My first of many international mission trips took me to Ethiopia.

One month before we departed for the mission trip, I woke up at about 2 am with chest pain and feeling weak. My husband called the ambulance, and I went to the emergency room. I was examined and was told that the test results showed that I had a heart attack. They admitted me to the ICU for five days and each time they spoke about a heart attack, I told them it was an attack alright but not a heart attack.

They ordered an angiogram procedure, which is where they inject a special dye into an artery through an arm or leg and it travels through to the coronary arteries. This test looks at the blood supply of the heart. It helps the Doctor to identify any narrowing inside the coronary arteries.

The results came back from that procedure and the doctor told me my heart was perfect. He said that if I had even a mild heart attack, there should be some scarred tissue, but everything was good. With all of this knowledge, he still didn't want to release me for my trip. Everything was paid for, and the professor did not want me to go without the doctor's approval. During that time in the ICU, I spent much time in prayer, as I needed to be certain God was sending me on this trip. Shortly after I was released and received the clearance from God to go.

One week before leaving, I went to a prayer breakfast where Katt Ker was the guest speaker. She spoke about her many visitations to heaven and seeing angels everywhere. This excited me because of all the things I've been through. I bought one of her books, "Revealing Heaven." I proceeded to have her autograph my copy and she said to me, "Normally I see two angels around people, but I see three around you. Are you going somewhere or about to do something?" I explained to her that I was going to Ethiopia the next week. She said to me one angel for power, one for protection, and the other one for peace. I thanked her and felt safe knowing that my angels were on duty.

On my way to Ethiopia on the plane I read her book and desired what she had. I told God I would like to see my angels and have visitations to heaven. (Be careful what you ask for you might just get it.)

In Ethiopia, we started preparing the ground where all the meetings were to take place. This is where all of the big names came down to have their crusades. We got resistance from the religious leaders of the city. They refused to give us light, so we had to go to the local electricity company for them to release the lights. We prayed and God delivered.

Everything came together for the weekend of the meeting. We commenced on Friday and thousands of people were in attendance. After the first session ended, the people stayed behind in the hot sun waiting for us to resume. There were countless miracles including blind eyes opening and people getting delivered from the devil. Only God alone gets the Glory! Hallelujah!

On Sunday morning, the last day of the crusade, the pastor and some of the men with him were resting for the night session. He had organized for me to go minister at a church. I was not pleased at all, the pastor sensed this, laid his hand on me, and said Lord anoint her, then he said go. I went reluctantly but was prepared for whatever God wanted me to do. He sent my friend from Canada and a native of Ethiopia with me.

Upon our arrival there was no interpreter, I was delighted and was ready to sit down and enjoy the service even though I didn't understand the language.

Afterward, the interpreter came, and I ministered as I was led by the Holy Spirit. I preached on the theme, "Back to Basics". The account expounded was about David and the Ark of Covenant, 2 Samuel 6. God's presence was felt in the church as He ministered to the people. This was more evident when the worshippers returned to do a second segment of worship. Although I did not understand the words they sang, the anointed could not be missed.

Thousands came from all over in whatever mode of transportation was available. The Lord moved mightily in the service. That night is ebbed in my memory. I saw the evidence of the word of God that says In Hebrew 2:4, "God also bearing them witness both with signs and wonders and with diver's miracles and gifts of the Holy Spirit according to His own will." This Word was manifested in our meetings! To God be all the Glory we take no glory for ourselves.

A brother was invited to close off the service in prayer. He called me up through the interpreter and said to me, "I saw a big caldron with oil in it, the Lord says He's anointing you for nations, and the nations will be calling you, just know that I God has sent you- mother of nations." The anointing was so strong that my knees started wobbling. The ladies who accompanied me held me up and then put me to sit down. I couldn't move even after the service was over, I sat there and greeted everyone.

We left from the rural areas of Sodo to Addis Ababa to continue the mission. We went to a church to minister, and after the pastor finished teaching, he asked us to go around and minister to the people as led by the Holy Spirit. A young lady was sitting by herself, and I went over to minister to her. Immediately as our eyes met, she started screaming and convulsing on the ground. Some men came and took her into a room where some ladies were. What happened there was not made known to me.

Then, immediately I was ushered into the spirit world. I saw waves like a current and it seemed as though I was not standing on the ground. My eyes opened to see the spirits of the people within the church, both good and bad. I could not feel my feet on the ground, therefore, I held on to the chairs and navigated my way to the front. I don't know how I reached behind the podium, but I stood there. It's like I was floating 3 feet off the ground. I was scared because I didn't understand what was happening to me. I asked God, "What is this? What's going on?" He said to me, "Don't you know that if I open your eyes to see your angels, you will also see demons?" I never thought about it that way so I said to Him, "ok God you will know when I'm ready." Immediately after submitting to God, I came back into my physical world.

I asked God to see my angels and He showed me a glimpse of what I asked for. The all-knowing God knew I was not ready for that assignment, and with that, I rested assured that He knew what was best for me.

God was not done with me yet! We were preparing to go home so we had a prayer of thanksgiving. We thank God for what He had done for the people of Ethiopia, and we were humbled that he chose us as his vessels to carry His glory. During the prayers, the pastor started ministering to me by way of the Holy Spirit. He told me, " I see you with binoculars looking into the enemy's camp strategically. I heard the Spirit of The Lord say you're a visionary and He is going to use you mightily for His glory! No one will get the Glory out of your life. Go back home and submit to the ministry you're in because where I'm taking you others will be submitting to you."

The pastor did not know that I was on the verge of leaving the ministry because I felt disconnected. I obeyed and when it was time to start the ministry God gave us in a vision, he released me from myself and the ministry I served for over 27 years. I still go to that ministry and support their function and they support us as well. There was a new pastor there by this time.

All the prophecies came to pass in my life. I have been to many African countries, European countries,

India, and the Caribbean! I have seen the Hand of God guiding me as I do the work, He has sent me to do. He said to Moses, "What is in your hands? Use it!!" I didn't know what I had until God used someone to reveal it to me. Now I do all for the Glory of God.

# Chapter 10

## Attacks

### *First Physical Attack*

I visited my doctor due to medical issues. Who referred me to a gynecologist who conducted some medical tests to determine the cause of my problems. He tried to perform a biopsy on me in his office, but the pain was unbearable. Therefore, he decided to perform a D&C at the hospital which is a procedure to remove tissue from the uterus to check for any abnormalities. Prior to going to the hospital, I asked some friends to pray for me. I refused to take this simple day procedure lightly because I sensed a dark presence hovering over me. While preparing me for the D&C, the prep nurse asked if I had low blood pressure, to which I replied, No. "She went ahead and got me prepared and sent me into the theatre. I stayed in there for far too long and my husband, along with my loved ones, came to the hospital because they were worried about the long hours I had spent in the theatre. My husband was extremely worried."

The doctor came out to talk to my husband about the surgery. My husband said that he knew something was wrong because the doctor's face was white as snow. He told my husband it was a difficult surgery and that during the procedure, my blood pressure went dangerously low. The doctors tried putting me on the breathing machine but couldn't get the tube down my throat, so they had to find another instrument that would fit. He reassured my husband that I was okay now. When the doctor told me the same story, I was glad to be alive. I later learned that I had actually stopped breathing during the surgery. After hearing this, I felt really sick. My husband took me home, and I rested. Thank God for answering prayers.

I went to see my doctor for a follow-up and the results of the DNC. She explained that if they had let me die, the whole hospital would have shut down; it's called "bench death," and it shouldn't have happened. This led me to believe the devil wanted me out. God protected His investment in me, and I am grateful. I give Him all the praise.

The cocoon and caterpillar stages are the most vulnerable for insects to infect the eggs of the butterfly with deadly viruses or parasites. This can disrupt the entire process of metamorphosis, causing the caterpillar to never become a butterfly and instead turn into a parasitic insect. Similarly, the devil injects evil seeds into humans, causing them to become morally corrupted.

This is one of the many attacks thrown at me from the pit of hell to abort my purpose and destiny. This was the first physical direct attack of the enemy on my life, others were spiritual warfare like; feeding me poison in my dream and pressing me while I was asleep. At this time the devil got physical with me to take me out when I entered the theater for that surgery. The devil is ferocious, brutal, deadly, and merciless. He intended that I did not come out alive but here is a more truth: as wicked as the devil is, his wicked acts cannot equate to the majesty of God's love for His people. If you are God's own, do all that is required of you, then go relax your mind.

## ***Second Attack***

The second physical attempt on my life from the devil was when my cholesterol level was elevated. I was advised to make some adjustments to my eating and incorporate exercises in my daily activities habits. I did blood work, but it was the summer period in Canada, so it was very hot and humid. This resulted in me consuming water regularly, and naturally a large intake of water causes one to urinate frequently. One night I was brushing my teeth in preparation for bed when suddenly, I felt my mouth was twisted and my saliva was coming out of my mouth. I screamed to my husband to come pray over me because I knew those were signs of a stroke. He rushed in and prayed over me, and all became normal again.

One Sunday morning, I got a call from my doctor which I didn't pick up because I was preparing for church. I had no doctor's appointment; therefore, I thought it was an automated service center from my doctor who was calling. Fifteen minutes later, the call came again, this time I picked up the phone and it was my doctor. She said the results from my lab work were back and the lab technician recommended that I be sent to the hospital as quickly as possible because my A1C level was 22; I didn't know what that meant. So, the next day I went to see my doctor, she showed me the result and explained some complicated things to me.

She asked me if I didn't feel dizzy the day before, I said no, then proceeded to recount the incident that happened while I was brushing my teeth. She explained that the lab work result requested that I be sent in for quick medication which would require me to be put on insulin. Being a born-again Christian, by faith she said, she was giving me three months to reverse whatever was wrong in my health. She cautioned me, if the condition was not reversed, she would have to have me hospitalized and placed on medication. I was given metformin which my body couldn't take because it made me nauseous. Then I was placed on a three-week medical checkup appointment, which I kept every appointment. Then after three weeks, I went in to see my doctor and my sugar level was back to normal and everything was fine with me. God healed me once again.

It's okay for us to be saved, live a good life, die, and go to heaven. However, when we step into our God-given purposes, all hell is on assignment to take us out. Our impact will be greater when we're out of our cocoons and our wings are properly dried. We are now ready to advance the Kingdom of God for His glory.

"Bless the Lord, O my soul; and forget not all His benefits. Who forgives all your iniquities, who heals all your diseases." Psalms 103:3

## *Attack through Rejection*

I was working in a factory, and one lady constantly came against me. If any other Christian said or did anything wrong, she would come to my station and say, "You Christians make me not want to get saved." I held my peace because I knew the Holy Spirit was convicting her. However, I was tired of her behavior, so I said to myself that I have to do something about my situation.

One Monday morning while my husband was taking me to work, I asked him if he could give me a week to go on a fast. He asked me what I was fasting for. I explained everything to him and added that I was asking God if I should go to a secular or Christian college. My husband's response was, "Seek ye first the Kingdom of God and everything will be added to you." He added that he would pay for my tuition. I said to him, "Honey, the Holy Spirit has spoken through you." I thanked him but was not sure how it was going to happen because we were struggling as a family to make ends meet. My husband paid for me to go to Canada Christian College. While preparing to go to school, the Holy Spirit spoke to me, saying that He was sending me there to meet someone. I didn't understand what the Holy Spirit was saying, but I pondered it in my heart.

I started going to school, meeting new people, and doing great. On my first exam, I earned 98%. I was excited and motivated. One day, the vice president's secretary came to me after meeting my daughter and me at a prophetic conference. I really didn't like this person, but God used her to start me on my journey to get my biblical credentials. She told me to get some certificates under my belt because the government wanted to see papers for me to do ministry. I guessed she was the person God wanted me to meet.

I decided I was going to become a licensed evangelist because I wanted to do prison ministry. This was one of my passions: to lead those who were incarcerated to Christ. Since I was not a pastor, the license would facilitate my access into prisons.

One of the requirements was that I should get a referral from my church. I informed my pastor of my plans, and he approved. I filled out the application and was given a date for an interview. On the day of my interview, the vice president of the college interviewed me. He started asking me a lot of questions, which I answered truthfully to the best of my abilities. By this time, he was writing and continued asking me questions. Finally, he said to me, "I cannot give you an ordained pastor's credential yet, but I can give you a lay pastor credential." I opened my mouth to say, "That's not what I came here for!" Like Zachariah in Luke 1, my mouth was shut! I tried to say something, but no words came out. By this time, I was scared and frustrated because I couldn't say a word. I knew my face was red because I could feel the hot blood rush up my neck to my face.

The vice president rolled up the paper he was writing on and handed it to me. I took it, and a "thank you" came out of my mouth. I was shocked! So I grabbed the paper and ran. I ran out of that office like a bullet to my husband, who was waiting for me in the parking lot. I told him all that transpired in the interview. He consoled me and said, "Never mind, you don't know what God is doing in your life." I said in a raised voice, "Pastor is going to say I am lying." I left everything in the hands of the Lord.

I went to see the pastor to let him know how the interview went. I told him what happened in the interview. He said to me, "You are lying; this thing is exactly what you have wanted for a long time" (this was because of the ministry I dreamt of). Additionally, he said I was forcing his hand. Now he had to tell the bishop and announce it to the church. I begged him not to, but he did it anyways. The way I was presented to the ministry, I was not celebrated.

One thing I saw was the hands of God leading and guiding me throughout all of this. I was ordained as a lay pastor at Canada Christian College. None of the pastors that didn't believe in what God was doing in my life, God didn't allow them to lay hands on me for ministry. God was and still is protecting His investments in me to bring forth his glory so I must go through my metamorphosis for this to happen.

After these attacks on my destiny, I had a dream that I went to hell. My husband told me he heard everything I was saying from 10:30 pm to 11:00 pm.

In the dream, I saw my husband and myself in hell. I witnessed demons whispering in his ears to discourage him. Eventually, he succumbed to the voices in his head and declared he was finished with the church. I responded, "It's okay, God called me to this assignment." He walked away, leaving me alone in the darkness.

A man in white clothing approached me and said, "Let me cover you because it's dangerous here." He laid me on the ground and covered me with a white sheet. Then, he began rubbing some black substance on my foot from what seemed like a reel. Suddenly, God opened my eyes, and I saw the man for what he truly was: a witch doctor with ashes and other markings on his face.

I rebuked him, and he disappeared, leaving me lying on the ground. As I looked up, I saw millions of demons floating overhead. Overwhelmed, I cried out to God, "This is overwhelming! I am going to bring Your glory here." I started singing, "JESUS, JESUS.... JESUS, JESUS.... how I love calling Your name." Suddenly, the place was filled with the glory of God.

John 1:15

And the light shines in the darkness, but the darkness could not overcome it.

After this, I found myself in another part of hell, this time protecting my family from the hands of the enemy. The groping hands of the demons were trying to grab my children and grandchildren. In the dream, I was furious, like a mother hen protecting her chicks. I say a small house, went inside, and cleansed it. I placed my family there to keep them safe from the demons. Then, I courageously jumped down to face the enemies. Can I tell you? Hell is dark, but the demons are darker than the darkness itself. All I saw were these dark shadows with red eyes looking at me with vengeance. They began throwing darts, their tips dipped in blood, at me. I noticed that the darts were dropping around me, as if they were hitting an invisible shield. There was an edge of protection around me. I pointed to the millions of shadowy figures surrounding me and said, "YOU CAN'T TOUCH THIS."

JOB1:10 Have you not put an edge of protection around him and his family and all that he has on every side?

Being rejected can be challenging but it can be more difficult when it comes from people who knows us for years and should be the ones to support and cheer us on. Sadly, most times our greatest support comes from strangers God sent to uplift us.

While rejection from our loved ones has caused heartbreak, let us not allow it to cause us to become bitter but better. Like the caterpillar, when an insect injects poison into the cocoon and it affects the caterpillar, instead of a butterfly a moth or parasitic butterfly comes out. Let us not allow bitterness to hinder our metamorphosis of becoming what God has created us to be. Let us allow the Healer of broken hearts to heal us from all rejection.

For every God given assignment, there is a destiny helper that will come alongside us to see the vision through without any strings attached. When God sends help it is guaranteed to make a difference between frustration and ease. These persons are strategically positioned to help.

Rejection in itself is sometimes God's way of cutting off what doesn't serve its purpose in our lives. Let's rejoice even when we don't understand.

# Chapter

# The In Between

Although necessary for our development, the things we've been through were very painful. They caused us pain and hurt us to the very core of our being.

God showed us the beginnings and the endings, and it seems glorious. What he did not show us was the in-between. Which contained struggles, setbacks, stop signs, ditches, midnight hours, abuses, refusals, feelings of inadequacy and the list goes on. Here in the in-between, the uncertainties overshadowed everything else. It overshadowed the beauty of our end product and the Glory of God. It makes the journey seem hard and tedious.

It's in the in-between where destinies are aborted or delayed. All because we never anticipated the part of our lives where we couldn't understand what was happening or we couldn't see our way out. We feel that we are all alone and God has somehow forsaken us.

God is timeless and He promises never to leave or forsake us. He is ever present at every moment of our lives if we would trust the process and trust the God who is processing us. It's the in-between, these two extremes, the beginning and ending that we are most excited about. The ending is when we are fully functioning in our purpose. We become one with our eternal existence, our why we were sent to earth. At the beginning we understand the assignment, so we get excited about the beginning and end.

It's the blank space when you can't hear His voice or the time when we doubt ourselves or even God. There were times when I asked God, are you sure that all things work together for my good? When I saw my son lying in that hospital bed not recognizing anyone, I asked God what is the good in all of this? This is the time when we have to trust God and believe he has our best interests at heart.

In these transitional periods where we can't see clearly, we can easily make decisions that will delay, derail, or abort our progress thus leaving us unfulfilled and unable to achieve our God-given assignments. We must be conscious that this is not the time to second guess what God is doing in your life. It's a time for us to trust the Most High to take us through these dark times.

The wait and the time may seem long in the in-between because God is perfecting what concerns us Psalms 138:8.

Some of us have sabotaged our process by overanalyzing where we are because it's not familiar with what we think should happen. Remember His thoughts are not our thoughts neither his ways our ways Isaiah 55:8-9. We analyzed the situation we were in and became stuck where we were. At this point there's no movement, no words from God, we feel like the heavens are made up of brass and you feel like giving up. We feel broken! This is exactly where God wants us to be. Mary had to break the

Alabaster box for the fragrance to come out. We have to be broken for that anointing to pour out of our lives.

The in-between came for Daniel when he was praying for 21 days. He could have given up in the first couple of days when he heard nothing from God. That would have aborted the plans of God not only for his life but also for Israel. In chapter 10 of Daniel, I paraphrase; from the first time you set your heart to understand the times and seasons that Israel was in, I have heard your heart, and your prayers were answered.

Some of us give up on the brink of our breakthroughs because we lack an understanding of our times and seasons, therefore we could abort our destinies and that of a whole nation.

To the human eyes, the in-between for the egg and the cocoon, seems to be a shell with no movement. This is the stage of the metamorphosis that is most crucial because if the butterfly doesn't go through it, it can die. Likewise, we, as children of the Most High

God, if we don't go through our process we become weak and ineffective in our ministry

The beautiful captivating film that we love dearly is developed in a dark room. Please before we shun the dark places in our lives, let us never forget that it's the dark places God develops us. If we can hold on a little longer, we will see the strength we have gained, the wisdom and passion for the things of God. Most of all our relationship and trust in God will be strengthened.

It was painful but necessary for us to be in the unknown and uncertainties. This helped us to know that God is the one who accomplishes His will in our lives. Thus, we learned to trust and obey God and thank him for his good pleasure and for us to affect our families, communities, cities, nations, and countries for His glory and His Honour.

To God be all the Glory!

# Chapter 11
# Launch Out

After the first dream about the Global Deliverance Ministries and my involuntary saying yes, some years went by, and I heard nothing from the Lord. Then the Lord told me to start a bible study and prayer meeting with my family. I immediately said no! A church is going to start from it. This was deposited in my spirit when a youth leader requested from the pastor, for them to have a prayer meeting at our home seeing what we were going through, with my parents passing and my son in the hospital from a car accident. I repeated what was told to me. We need to guard our ear gates against what we hear and listen to because when it gets into our spirits, it's hard to get rid of it.

My husband and I attended a conference hosted by one of our pastor friends. There was a prophetess who was the minister for the weekend. We attended on the

Saturday where she ministered to us, she was so precise that we knew it was undeniably God.

After the service, the pastor asked me to pray for the prophetess which I did under the unction of the Holy Spirit. After the meeting was over, she sought me out and asked me if I would like to join a prayer meeting, she was commencing. I was free on the day, so I said yes, not knowing it was a set-up from God.

The first time we gathered it was seven of us in attendance. We started in the house of the prophetess. The plan was to rotate the meeting in each of our homes. My house was the second to host the prayer meeting. During the meeting, the Spirit of The Lord spoke through the prophetess and said "This is where the Ark of The Covenant stays.

The Ark of The Covenant is also known as the Ark of God or the Ark of Testimony. It represents the presence of Yahweh as a protector and guardian for the Israelites. It was this presence of God that resided in our home. Blessings started flowing in my house, which was also manifested through changes in my children. My husband, who was not working at the time received a call from a friend who asked if he needed a job. He responded- yes. The friend introduced him to a man who owned a chalking company where he trained my husband to do waterproofing and fire-stopping. My husband started working in construction and began making good money. Today he and his boss are like brothers. To God be all the Glory.

In short order, the upper part of my house was no longer sufficient to seat the amount of people who were coming to the prayer meetings. We had to go to the basement which was unfinished at the time. One of the ladies attending the prayer meetings gave us 40 chairs and a pastor gave me a podium.

"I visited with this pastor before registering my ministry, as the Lord spoke to me and instructed me to do so before someone else used the name. Although I obeyed, I still didn't have the desire to actively participate in the ministry. As long as someone else was leading it, in this case, the prophetess, I was okay with that."

There were days when we had over forty people in my basement. We fasted and prayed, and many deliverances took place. People who came sick left healed. The presence of the Lord was very evident in my home. Many churches were birthed out of these meetings and today still actively advancing the Kingdom of God.

On Wednesday mornings at 10 am, my house is always filled with people which is surprising for a midweek day. To be a part of this, I worked double shifts to get my Wednesdays off from work because I didn't want to miss a day. During these meetings, the presence of God was so strong that many Miraculous signs and wonders followed the preaching of the Word.

During the fasting service, my husband prepared a large pot of soup for the attendees. They would put money in an envelope to buy the necessary ingredients. However, in a vision, the Lord revealed to my husband that the soup was complimentary and did not require any payment. My husband would get up early and prep the soup and I would finish it. He would sometimes come home early and be a part of the service.

Different ministers would come and share in the prayer meeting. Often, they would minister to me, saying the Lord said, "It is time," while others would say they saw a green light over me with the words "Go" written above it. I dreaded going down to the prayer meeting and sometimes stayed to watch over the soup. I didn't want anyone to pick me out and tell me anything else.

"I used to be content with serving others from behind the scenes, going on missions and ministering around Canada, as long as I could do the ministry and then leave. But as I received more prophecies over my life, I became more sensitive to the fact that God was speaking to me.

I believe that God has the power to transform anyone or anything for His glory. All He requires from us is our obedience and willingness to follow His guidance."

I became tired of receiving prophetic messages, but once again I found myself involuntarily agreeing to one. A prophet helped us find a place to house our ministry, conducting all the necessary investigations and providing me with all the information he had gathered. The rent for the place was $220 per month, to be paid quarterly.

My husband and I could manage so it was comfortable for us, so we secured the place to start in October 2010.

Despite serving in a ministry for a long time in different capacities we didn't know how to structure a ministry and we didn't have anyone who would come alongside us to mentor us in any way. We went to our then-pastor from the church we were attending and relayed everything that was happening as he already knew about the prayer meeting. We told him the expected day we intended to start the ministry. He had a service for us and blessed and sent us off. We had challenges seeing that my husband and I were first-time ministers of the gospel in our families. We were in total reliance on the Holy Spirit.

Just when we were settling into the ministry and could afford to pay the rent, had our first baptism of 4 persons to God be the Glory, the city served us notice because they were going to renovate the building which meant we had no option but to move. We were too comfortable relying on our own strength and the word says" Upon this rock I God will build my church. We found a place that cost way more than the previous one. The payment was challenging but we trust in the providence of God.

Our membership was drastically reduced to only a handful, mostly young people. As a result, my husband and I were left to handle the mortgage payments on our own. We had our responsibilities to attend to during this difficult time, but we had no choice but to trust in the One who sent us. Through it all, I learned that He may not come when you want Him, but He's always on time.

Sometimes we were unsure of where the money to pay for our church mortgage would come from. However, God always provides in unexpected ways. Whether it's through someone who says God told them to give us money, or unexpected funds in our account from the government who underpaid us for something. We learned that we can always count on God to come through for us.

My husband and I faced uncertainties while running our ministry. We had no prior training in how to structure it and often had disagreements on our respective roles. He saw me as the visionary and I saw him as the pastor, but we didn't fully understand our different functions, which led to conflicts.

"There have been many instances where we were on the verge of shutting down the ministry, but each time we reached that point, God would send someone to support and strengthen us. Another time, when we were about to give up and close the church, God spoke to me and said, "You didn't start it therefore you can't finish it."

Since then, I have stopped trying to control God's plans and surrendered to His will. John 15:16 states that it is not us who chose Him, but rather He chose and appointed us to bear fruit that will last. This means that we can ask the Father for anything in Jesus' name, and He will grant it to us.

We have had many encounters with people in our lives who were not good for us. Spiritually, we were easy prey for them to abuse us. However, God always made a way for us to escape and helped us rise above our struggles. Although it was painful, it was necessary for our growth. I am sure that the caterpillar in its cocoon went through growing pains because of the changes it went through. This helped to build our character and made us who we are today.

God created us to be what He intended us to be, not necessarily what we wish to become. During the transformation from cocoon to butterfly, many people give up on their destiny due to the pressure and challenges that come with the process. However, it is only through this process that the butterfly ultimately emerges. Nevertheless, if the wings of the butterfly do not develop properly, it cannot fly so it will stay there and die, or some insect will eat it. At this point in our lives and ministry, things are crucial. They can either make or break us. The Global Deliverance Ministries has been established with various ministries under it. We have been instructed by our Father to make the ministry a safe place for the abused, cast-offs, downtrodden, and those who are lost. When they come to us, they should not be further abused, but instead, we should lead them towards God for healing. Our ministry is a secure and peaceful place.

# Chapter 12

## Covid

My husband and I were fostering two young children through an agency. One child was in senior kindergarten, while the other was not yet of school age. One day, the eldest child came home from school complaining of a headache. We gave her some children's Tylenol, thinking that it might have been caused by her crying the night before. Their visit with their biological mother for the weekend had been canceled.

The following morning, my daughter was feeling better, and everything seemed normal. However, my husband, who was the primary worker, took her to school and picked her up that day. Later in the evening, he started coughing persistently. We decided to book an online appointment for a Covid PCR test, but unfortunately, I only filled out one form and missed my husband's. We found out the next day when we received the appointment that only I had an appointment. My husband had to book another appointment for the following day.

"We didn't think much of it, so we didn't sleep in separate rooms. On the day of his appointment, my results came in, and it turned out that I was negative. We were grateful to God and assumed that my husband must have just had a cold or some other bug since I tested negative. We slept in the same bed that night. During the night I felt an unusual pain all over my body. I wondered what that was. I brushed it off as nothing.

The following day my husband got his results, and he tested positive. All this while we were taking care of the asymptomatic children. A public health nurse called and told me to quarantine my husband, which I did. This left me alone to take care of the children and him.

The devil gave me another blow when my daughter downstairs caught COVID as well. Now, I had to take care of the whole household. I took the necessary precautions because where I worked at Christian Horizons there was an outbreak, and all the people whom we supported, and the majority of the staff were infected with Covid. I was trained on how to wear my PPE and protect myself and others. By this time, I was infected with Covid and didn't know it. I wasn't coughing or anything, just feeling a little tired. All the work I was doing explained this.

The agency that we do foster for told me to go get the girls tested, which I did. The next day I got the results for the girls, and it was positive. The public health nurse called me and told me to quarantine myself from everyone. Since my husband and everyone else were positive he could take care of them. He didn't have it bad so he was able and with the support from family, friends, and the agency we foster for he could manage.

By this time, I was so weak I dropped down, it's at this time I started coughing and felt pain in my lungs. There were days that I didn't know where I was. I begged my husband not to take me to the hospital because of all the horror stories I heard. If I had been to the hospital I wouldn't be here today.

My family pulled out the home remedies to help me to fight this virus. I couldn't eat much. Just a little sip of tea or juice or maybe soup. Any movement I would cough and any activity I would go into uncontrollably coughing. I didn't eat or drink much but all my body fluids I was urinate out. I was becoming dehydrated, and my husband had to force me to drink something.

At this point, I blocked out and didn't know night from day. Sleep was the only thing I wanted to do.

This was one of the worst seasons of my metamorphosis. I saw my health declining every day, I felt like I was dying. I was only 59 years old in 2020 and was dying. My husband called my children to come see me because he didn't think I was going to make it.

One day in the middle of the day, whether I was asleep or awake I don't know. I saw in a vision two doors one marked DEATH DOOR on the right and the other marked GRAVE on the left. I started walking towards the death door it was so peaceful and that propelled me to go on. On my way the reality of the unknown hit me, so I stopped, slightly turned around, and looked up as if I was looking at a tall person which I couldn't see. I said to the invisible person that I felt was there. God before I go let me ask you one question; are you for real or are you a figment of my imagination? As soon as the question came out of my mouth a strong ball like electricity hit me in my chest with a big whoosh. The Lord blew breath into me because I took a breath and for once in days I could inhale without coughing.

The second question I asked Him was God, you told me to start a network and I have not started it yet; are you going to stand there and make this thing take me out? Immediately another big ball of electricity woosh hit my chest again it caused me to take a deep breath which I couldn't do without coughing uncontrollably.

Before this encounter, God told me in a dream to start a network. He gave me the name of the network and the color to be used for the logo. I did not need to ask anyone for confirmation or clarification because the directive was as plain as day. This I held up to Him to remind him of His words. Isaiah 43:27 "Put me in remembrance, let us plead together; declare thou that thou may be justified."

The last thing I said to God was that I just bought a house with the intention of taking my son who was brain-injured home from the long-term care facility. I said I haven't completed the house yet, what is going to happen to my son if I die? My children will say that their dad can't handle the situation. I said to him, what is going to happen to my son? I repeated this more frantically. Immediately another big ball of electricity hit my chest, this one was the strongest whoosh. God blew life back into me. The vision continued. I saw myself standing in the spirit realm when a golden armour came on me and one of the biggest golden swords dropped into my hand.

Although the sword was big it was very light in my hand.

In that vision, I saw a big black piece of blob crawling on the ground towards me. I took the sword and chopped off its head. Following this I saw a little white one. At first, I thought the white represented purity, so I was going to spear it, but I remembered that Covid has variants, so I destroyed it as well.

That encounter with God Himself made me look at life differently. I got to know Him specially. After all this I got up and sat up in my bed, I was able to take my time and go downstairs and sit in the sun with my son. My life was transformed because of this encounter! No one and I mean no one can tell me God is not real.

After I tested negative for COVID, it took several months for my body to recover. It's by the grace of God ***I'm alive today.***

I can say like Paul. I am persuaded that neither death nor life nor angels nor principalities nor powers nor things present nor things to come nor height nor depths nor any other creatures shall be able to separate me from the love of God in Christ Jesus. Selah

This is part of the process of my metamorphosis and countless others as well, where God processes us from being immature (babes). Some changes required us to be on the potter's wheel, some through the valley, some through the floods but all through His precious blood.

Our changes are a continual process throughout our lifetime. He will never leave us comfortless.

"We all with open faces beholding as in a glass the glory of the Lord are changed into the same image from glory to glory even as by the Spirit." (2 Corinthians 3:18)

# Conclusion

Once the chrysalis begins splitting, the butterfly emerges within seconds. The butterfly then spreads its wings and expands its abdomen for several minutes. It takes 90-120 minutes for the wings to be dried enough for the butterfly to take short flights. The butterfly is best ready for the work it's sent to do in the world if it stays for 24 hours before doing anything.

Timing is very important in our metamorphosis. If we come out of our cocoon too soon, we can die and abort our destiny. If we stay too long the possibility is the cocoon can't hold us and we could die in transition thus aborting all possibilities of our becoming.

When the butterflies are ready, they do more for us than beautify our gardens. They pollinate our plants when their bodies collect pollen and carry them to other plants. This helps fruits vegetables and flowers to produce new seeds.

I give God the Glory for where I am in my becoming who he has called me to be not what I wanted to be. There will always be major differences when we do it God's way. Although we have situations along the way that seem impossible for us to overcome, we have a Father who is ever present, ever faithful and He's benevolent. Each day He gives new mercies, He sees, and provides. Most of all He is love. John 3:16

Only God alone will get the Glory out of my life and out of this book. He commanded me to write to help others in their metamorphosis.

I thank God for the journey, today I'm at a good place knowing and understanding who I am in Him. Understanding that I was sent complete to accomplish my purpose here on earth. I understand the authority that I have, being seated with God In heavenly places at his right hand of power and authority.

I thank God for entrusting me and my husband to lead the Global Deliverance International Ministries. It is now established and fully functioning under the care of the Holy Spirit. We have branches in Pakistan and Kenya and many collaborations around the world.

The network He told me to start, which I reminded him of when I was dying of COVID-19, is finally finished and about to be aired on all social media platforms.

Finally, He has retired me from my secular job and made me an entrepreneur with my daughter and husband over a multimillion-dollar business. What I don't know about He sends someone to help me get it done. In this instance, God uses my daughter to spearhead this business venture.

It has been a journey. If I had to do it over again, I would make better choices and do it from a place of being finished understanding God and his plans and purposes for my life to bring forth His praise and glory in my becoming.

# About the Author

ANNETTA DRUMMOND is an entrepreneur, marriage, and life coach with the mandate to reform the minds of people towards God. Connecting mankind to His original glorious place in destiny in all areas in God. She took up the mantle of her call at a young age. She's married to DERVIN DRUMMOND for 43 years; blessed with 5 awesome children and 7 Godly grandchildren. In 2017 the Apostle called and mandated her husband, Pastor DERVIN

DRUMMOND, Senior pastor of Global Deliverance Ministries in Canada. She is also the CEO of Kingdom Konnect Network. Since 2003 until date; she has been going around the world impacting and teaching God and His ways to thousands of people in places like Ethiopia, India Cameron, Kenya, Holland, the UK, Ghana, Gambia, the Caribbean, and many more. She is a true kingdom builder who ensures that Jesus Christ is exemplified in all that she does, thus creating a legacy in advancing the Kingdom of God on Earth. She is a pacesetter, nation builder, trailblazer, and an apostolic arrowhead in her generation.

# ANNETTA DRUMMOND

Made in the USA
Middletown, DE
27 July 2024